Beginning to END

Wax To Crayon

A Buddy Book

by

Julie Murray

ABDO
Publishing Company

VISIT US AT
www.abdopublishing.com

Published by ABDO Publishing Company, 4940 Viking Drive, Edina, Minnesota 55435.

Copyright © 2007 by Abdo Consulting Group, Inc. International copyrights reserved in all countries. No part of this book may be reproduced in any form without written permission from the publisher. Buddy Books™ is a trademark and logo of ABDO Publishing Company.

Printed in the United States.

Coordinating Series Editor: Sarah Tieck
Contributing Editor: Michael P. Goecke
Graphic Design: Maria Hosley
Cover Photograph: Photos.com
Interior Photographs/Illustrations: Media Bakery, Photos.com, William Thomas Cain/Getty Images (pages 15, 17, 19, 20, 21)
Special thanks to Sydney Hosley for original artwork (page 6).

Library of Congress Cataloging-in-Publication Data

Murray, Julie, 1969–
    Wax to Crayon / Julie Murray.
        p. cm. — (Beginning to end)
    Includes index.
    ISBN-13: 978-1-59679-915-8
    ISBN-10: 1-59679-915-3
        1. Crayons—Juvenile literature. 2. Paraffin wax—Juvenile literature. I. Title.

TS1268.M87 2006
688—dc22

                                                                    2006019909

Table Of Contents

What Are Crayons Made Of?

Many people use crayons. Children use them to color pictures. Adults use them for art, too.

Crayons come in many colors and styles. New crayon colors are created all the time.

Children use crayons to draw and color.

5

There are basic crayon colors, such as red, green, and blue. There are also more unusual colors. These include **neon**, **glitter**, and **metallic** crayons. Do you know how crayons are made?

A picture drawn with crayons.

Crayons come in a variety of colors. Some are shiny and metallic. Some are bright and neon.

A Starting Point

There are two main **ingredients** used to make most crayons. These ingredients are **paraffin** wax and **pigment**.

Paraffin wax forms a crayon's body. Pigment gives a crayon its color. To make a crayon, paraffin wax and pigment are mixed together.

Different pigment combinations change the color of the paraffin.

At The Factory

Crayons are a man-made product. They are manufactured in a **factory**.

One of the most famous crayon makers is Crayola. The Crayola Factory is located in Easton, Pennsylvania.

A company named Binney and Smith sold the first Crayola crayons in 1903. At that time, a pack of eight crayons cost five cents.

The name Crayola comes from the words *craie* and *oleaginous*. *Craie* is a French word that means "chalk." The word *oleaginous* describes **paraffin** wax, which can be oily.

Paraffin is used to make some candles.

FUN Facts
Did you know...

Norwegian—Blå

English—Blue

French—Bleu

Spanish—Azul

Dutch—Blauw

… Crayon labels come in more
than 11 languages.

… In the early 1900s,
there were eight colors
in a box of crayons.
Today, the biggest box
has 120 colors.

Blue Orange Yellow Green Brown Violet Black Red

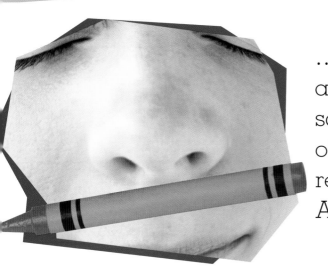

... Yale University did a study on smells. The scent of a crayon is one of the top 20 most recognized smells by American adults!

... It takes less than 10 minutes for a factory to make one crayon.

faster than baking a cake

Melting Pot

Paraffin wax comes from crude oil. It can be melted and formed into any shape. But first it must go through several steps.

At a crayon factory, paraffin wax is mixed with pigment. Pigments are mixed to make many different colors.

When the mixture is heated, the wax melts to a liquid. Heat makes the wax and the pigment blend together.

A worker adds red pigment to a kettle of hot wax. This mixture will make red crayons.

After the wax has melted, it is time to shape the crayon. Crayons are shaped using a mold. A mold has many crayon-shaped holes. A machine pours the colored hot wax into the holes. One mold can make more than 2,400 crayons at once!

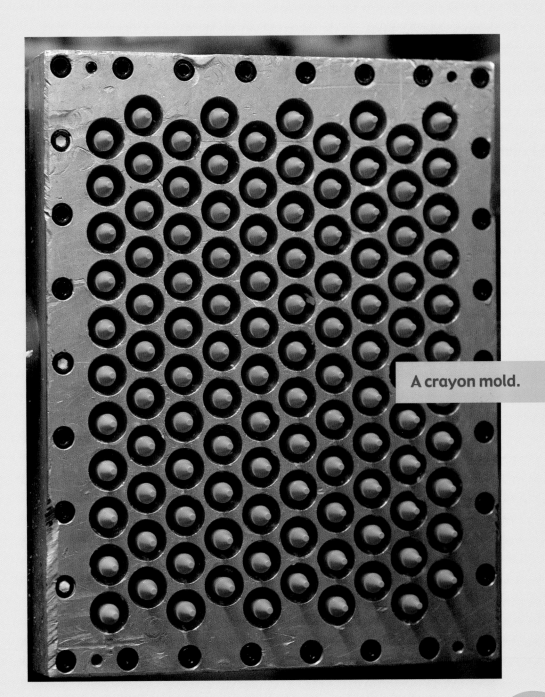

A crayon mold.

From Factory To Box

Next, the crayons cool. This takes between four and seven minutes. When the crayons are cool, a machine knocks them out of the mold.

After this, a person checks the crayons. Next, the crayons are taken to another machine. This machine puts a label on each crayon.

A factory worker places crayons into a packaging machine.

Different colored crayons are sorted to be put into boxes.

After each crayon has a label, it is put into a box. Then, the box is taken to a store for people to buy.

Next time, you pull a crayon out of a box, think about how it got there.

Crayons are put into boxed sets.

Can You Guess?

Q: What company first sold Crayola crayons in 1903?

A: Binney and Smith

Q: Who gave crayons their name?

A: Alice Binney

Important Words

crude   the raw, or unrefined, state.

factory   a business that uses machines to help with work.

glitter   sparkly flakes often used in crafts.

ingredient   a part of a mixture.

metallic   metal, such as gold or silver.

neon   color that is extremely bright.

paraffin   a type of wax.

pigment   a substance used as coloring.

Web Sites

To learn more, visit ABDO Publishing Company on the World Wide Web. Web site links about this topic are featured on our Book Links page. These links are routinely monitored and updated to provide the most current information available.

www.abdopublishing.com

Index